Winter
Wishes

Written by: M.H. Clark

Illustrated by: Cécile Metzger

This season I wanted to give you a gift—
something too big to wrap... so that's what this is.

Because wishes aren't things you can tie with a bow,
and once you have made them, they grow and grow.

And if these ones turned out especially huge...
it's because they are heartfelt. Because they're for you.

I'm wishing you sparkle and spirit and cheer
and good things to come that will last you all year.

And anticipation that hangs in the air.
And treats that are sweeter because they are shared.

I'm wishing surprises you didn't expect,
and wonders you can't quite imagine just yet.

And moments of magic you cannot explain
that make you feel just like a child again.

And favorite traditions passed down through the years
that keep loved ones close, even when they aren't here.

I'm wishing you moments of joy so complete
that it shines in your eyes and it brightens your cheeks...

And letters and presents and hugs from good friends
who remind you you're treasured, again and again.

Then, I'm wishing you moments of stillness and rest—
quiet time just to savor the things you love best.

And a soft sense of wonder in dark wintry nights
that makes things feel peaceful and hopeful and right.

Because winter's a season of light in the heart,
and you have a spirit that shines like a star...

And the gift that you give just by being yourself
is brighter and rarer than anything else.

Which is why the last wish that I'm making for you
is the wish that each one of these wishes comes true.

Here's to you, and your presence, your generousness,
the way things are better because you exist.

I'm so grateful to know that this newest of years
will bring more time together, and days we'll hold dear.

And these warm thoughts won't stop with the coming of spring—
I'll still be here wishing you every good thing...

Because someone as special and cherished as you
should have joy and delight to last all the year through.

COMPENDIUM®
live inspired

Written by: M.H. Clark
Illustrated by: Cécile Metzger
Edited by: Bailey Vega
Art Directed by: Chelsea Bianchini

ISBN: 978-1-970147-96-4

1st printing. Printed in China with soy inks on FSC®-Mix certified paper.

Create meaningful moments with gifts that inspire.

CONNECT WITH US
live-inspired.com | sayhello@compendiuminc.com

   @compendiumliveinspired
#compendiumliveinspired